# RESTORATIVE JUSTICE: OUTSIDE THE INSIDE OF THE STATE OF ILLINOIS

## Kurtis M. Williams

*"YOU CAN'T GO BACK AND CHANGE THE BEGINNING, BUT YOU CAN START WHERE YOU ARE AND CHANGE THE ENDING."*

C.S. Lewis

# Table of Contents

## Forward

As one who has practiced, studied and taught a variety of subjects involving the administration of justice, it has always been the topic of incarceration and rehabilitation that was top of mind. During my 12 years as a senior juvenile probation officer, my assignment included several years as the department's Social History Investigator. As such, it was my job to arrive at a set of recommendations for the disposition of cases involving delinquency and to defend those recommendations to the judges, prosecutors and defense counsel. Over time, I recommended that these young people be sent to foster homes, group homes, treatment programs, psychiatric hospitals, and to the Department of Corrections. In addition, as a probation officer, I dealt with the 'before' and 'after' of those dispositions.

Kurtis Williams, the author of this treatise, was one of those youth. His life story offers a deep dive into the best—and worst—of what our system had to offer. At the time, I considered him one of my success stories. That changed and the young man I knew then is the man serving life in prison and hoping against hope for a grant of clemency.

What you will read in these pages—a very detailed and comprehensive proposal—is his offering to the world of a program that he truly believes could be life-changing for the incarcerated *and* for the public that pays for and lives with the consequences of a correctional system that often does the opposite of its name. It is grounded in his experiences over 28+ years of incarceration and informed by personal experience.

In 1981, in his remark at the University of Nebraska, Chief Justice Warren Burger made the case for prison reform, aptly labeled *"More Warehouses, or Factories with Fences[1]"*. Watching the country undertake billions of dollars in prison construction, the Chief Justice believed that prisons should be focused on education and training. It is in his spirit that Kurtis puts forward his version of reform.

While there has been much progress in the development of community-based alternatives to incarceration, and more attention paid to the needs of 'returning citizens, Kurtis' hope is that his proposal will be given serious consideration by all those affected, both inside and outside the prison system of the State of Illinois and beyond.


Kerry D. Knodle

Rockford, Illinois

October 2024

---

[1] https://www.cia.gov/readingroom/docs/CIA-RDP83M00914R002400040008-8.pdf

## Acknowledgements

The author, Kurtis M. Williams, would first like to thank Illinois Representative Maurice West (D-Rockford), his Chief of Staff, Jeremy Ennis, and Sergeant Reyes of the Dixon Correctional Center, formerly a correctional officer, for making it possible for this author to engage in discussions about rehabilitative techniques and applications. Additionally, thanks go to them for ensuring the author's safety during the study and compilation of this book. Thank you, Sgt. Reyes.

To Correctional Officer Hollins: Thank you for your vast understanding of life, your service to our country, and, along with Sgt. Reyes, for your dedication. Thank you both for your service and for your ability, Officer Hollins, to multitask and accomplish things efficiently.

To my editor, Kerry D. Knodle, who has been involved in restorative justice since I was a troubled kid in a group home, caught with pot, and placed in your care as a probationer: Without your steadfast, quiet calm and assertiveness, this would not be possible. Thank you for allowing me to help create a program that may change the application of restorative justice for millions of Illinoisans.

To Holly Michelle Williams: You are incredible, loving, and kind. I am grateful to be your dad. I love you.

To Governor Pritzker: I would like to acknowledge the will for change that I have witnessed from behind bars. Even as an interstate compact in-custody offender, not serving time for your state but for Florida, I realize that with this program, if it ever lands on your desk, you as the Governor of Illinois may actually do something with it on behalf of Illinoisans, such as veterans, retirees, business owners, farmers, and victims. The Illinois Constitution requires that all offenders be restored to productive citizenship, and this includes victims of crime as well.

I also acknowledge that this program may not reach your desk, but possibly that of an Illinois successor. I hope and pray that if not in my lifetime, then in yours, you will convey this program to the people of this state on their behalf and on behalf of crime victims.

## Dedication

The author would like to dedicate this book to his beautiful daughter, Holly M. Williams, and to his editor, Kerry D. Knodle, who has been and continues to be essential in Kurtis' life, providing hope, clemency, and daily motivation. Thank you for being the father figure I never had before you came into my life.

To the "soon-to-be Warden" of Dixon Correctional Center, Sgt. D. Reyes: This book is dedicated to you for your commitment to fairness, justice, and routine with authority. You exemplify these values, which you first learned as a sergeant in the Army and now apply in the Illinois Department of Corrections. I listened to you as you exercised your strengths and authority in the face of challenges, such as dealing with prisoners suffering from drug-induced psychosis, particularly those addicted to K-2 and other substances. You were always calm in the face of every storm I witnessed, and there were many. For this reason, I hope and pray that people like you, Sgt. Reyes, will run programs like this one, which are essential to the responsible use of tax dollars dedicated to restorative justice.

This book is also dedicated to every citizen in Illinois who has been a victim of crime, and to the judges who strive for better justice on their behalf.

## About the Author

Kurtis M. Williams is an interstate compact inmate serving a natural life sentence in the state of Illinois based on a wrongful conviction in the state of Florida. However, he accepted a no-contest plea to be closer to his daughter, Holly M. Williams, whom he loves and adores. He was born and raised in Illinois, spending his youth between Rockford and Chicago. He has experienced over 28 placements, including foster care, residential facilities, group homes, institutions, and impact programs throughout Illinois during his childhood and young adulthood.

Kurtis has been in prison since March 13, 1996, serving nearly 28 consecutive years. During this time, he has fully paid off his child support through his work and efforts on his daughter's behalf and has earned over 30 certificates. He is a paralegal and the author of a fourteen-book series of Sudoku trivia books, as well as the first and second editions of *Poems from Within*. Kurtis has firsthand knowledge of effective rehabilitative programming. He has seen hundreds of inmates return to prison after being released with only $10 in their pocket, without any certifications, accreditations, or vocational training. The programs currently in place are all non-accredited and are taught by rotating counselors or correctional officers who juggle multiple responsibilities. These programs, such as anger management, conflict resolution, and lifestyle redirection, fail to make any real rehabilitative impact on the offender population, society, or victims of crime throughout Illinois.

Kurtis has a unique perspective on the inefficiencies of such programming and how it misuses tax dollars intended for rehabilitation. He has created a program aimed at class three and four felony offenders that works through plea agreements at the discretion of sentencing judges, state attorneys, and legislators. The program directly benefits victims of crime, retirees, veterans, business owners, farmers, and communities at large.

Kurtis is not claiming to know everything about rehabilitation, but he believes that involving veterans, retirees, business owners, farmers, and programs like the Rosecrance Domestic Battery Prevention with Drug Impact and Morgue Impact Program—under a construct of accreditation and certification—will be a starting point for Illinois. Some may argue that he lacks the university credentials to propose such a program. However, Kurtis has been involved in the criminal justice system since he was five years old. He has been shot, stabbed, and victimized by crime, and he himself grew up as a criminal. He does not claim to be perfect but is offering something back to society that is missing: the opportunity for victims, retirees, veterans, and citizens to have a hand in restorative justice as it directly affects them, without additional costs through appropriations.

Kurtis has researched the details and found that the program will pay for itself through already allocated funds, the Federal Rehabilitation Act, the Federal Infrastructure Bill, and green energy grants from the federal government.

Kurtis is not expecting to be freed. He is a man of faith and lives according to his deep-seated faith in God and family. He understands that the program he is proposing will not affect him, as he would never be eligible for it. He will be filing his clemency petition with the State of Florida Clemency Commission in the hope that he can help change the landscape of restorative justice programming during his lifetime. Kurtis knows it will take courage for politicians to adopt a program that affects every voter. However, not adopting the program would mean saying "no" to victims of crime, retirees, veterans, morgue impact programming, the Rosecrance Domestic Battery Prevention program, farmers, business owners, and judges who lack discretionary tools like this program.

Kurtis is hopeful that he can help save one victim of crime at a time by reducing recidivism through true restorative justice. He currently resides at Dixon Correctional Center in northern Illinois, in the custody of the Illinois Department of Corrections. He is working on a book entitled *The Young Rockfordian*, a fictional novel about a young man unsuccessfully involved in the criminal justice system through foster care, group homes, residential placements, and institutions. After being convicted of auto theft, he enters a new program called the "Restorative Justice Outside the Inside Program of Illinois" through a plea agreement.

Kurtis' works are available on Amazon.com. or by scanning the QR code below:

## THE QUESTION

The question that every citizen sitting at home asks is the same question Kerry Knodle and Caitlin Downy asked me during a visit to the Dixon Correctional Center in Northern Illinois: "Why should taxpayers want to pay for a new program related to prisoners and their plea agreements from court cases throughout Illinois, and why now?"

Currently, taxpayers pay no less than $18,500 to $24,000 per year for each inmate serving time in the Illinois Department of Corrections (IDOC). Taxpayers are assured that, without meaningful programs or training, 98% of all offenders admitted to the IDOC will return and recidivate, costing our society and its taxpayers even more money as these offenders cycle back into prison.

As a routine, offenders currently in custody are employed but not certified in any job capacity within the IDOC until after they prove themselves by working in the inmate dietary department. Even then, due to lockdowns and staff shortages, it's virtually impossible to enter, let alone complete, a certified program within any IDOC facility. Upon completion of their sentence, offenders are given a bus ticket and $10. They are either forced to enter a halfway house (which taxpayers already pay for, along with associated medical costs) or parole to a family or friend's home, penniless. In both scenarios, they become a burden and a threat to the community because they remain untrained, undisciplined, and still criminal thinkers. Thus, the $18,500-$24,000 taxpayers spent on each offender does nothing for them, their families, their neighbors, the courts, or society—other than preparing the offender to offend again.

This program, unlike any other you've heard or read about, involves you, your neighbors, the courts, business owners, farmers, retirees, and veterans, both inside and outside the system, as a voice on behalf of crime victims and advocates for the proper appropriation of your tax dollars. Naturally, taxpayers will question whether sex offenders, murderers, or rapists will be eligible for such a program. The clear and certain answer is no. Only offenders who have entered a plea negotiation through a state's attorney and received a judge's approval will be allowed to participate. This includes only those convicted of class three and four felonies. Many of these crimes affect numerous victims, and the program focuses on addressing their needs.

We call this program **Restorative Justice: Outside the Inside of Illinois** because it is about you, as a representative citizen, having a say in how your tax dollars work for your community. It aims to restore victims of crime to some semblance of restitution through the rehabilitative work of offenders who victimized them or society at large.

The idea of offering minimum wages for two years at 50 hours per week is new and revolutionary, especially when you consider that half of those wages will go directly to crime victims. One-quarter of the wages will go toward child support, court fines, and the costs associated with the conviction process, while the final quarter will be saved for the offender upon successfully completing the program.

This program includes society—through retirees, veterans, farmers, and business owners—within the appropriations tied to that $24,000 you pay to incarcerate, with the expectation of success and a much lower likelihood of recidivism. The federal government has awarded all 50 states infrastructure money, which includes funds for community centers for rehabilitation throughout Illinois. The brick and mortar of these centers won't cost taxpayers anything. In fact, the state of Illinois, under this program, will be required to purchase abandoned parcels of land in participating communities, where small homes built by program participants will be developed. This initiative will increase property values in those communities.

Taxpayers should be thrilled that their felony-convicted neighbor living in a small home nearby is employed full-time, pays taxes, and is certified in over nine fields related to home building or gardening. For the first time, the convicted felon will have something to lose if they reoffend! It's unlikely that anyone who is successfully trained and certified in nine expert fields with a full-time job would risk reoffending. It's also worth noting that the Rosecrance drug and domestic violence treatment programs will be incorporated into this initiative, further rehabilitating offenders and restoring them as productive citizens of Illinois.

If you, the taxpayer, do not have a voice and cannot direct your tax dollars to effective use, then you are allowing politicians to continue wasting the $18,500-$24,000 per year you pay for the same class 3 and 4 felons—who are merely waiting to be paroled so they can reoffend under the current status quo.

This book is for our society, for our people, including victims, lawyers, judges, business owners, farmers, veterans, retirees, and John and Jane Q. Taxpayer—who now have a voice and a literal book to present to their legislators to ask the question: Why not?

## Welcome to the Restorative Justice Outside the Inside Illinois Program (RJOTIP)

It is the goal of the State of Illinois to first restore all victims impacted by the crimes attributed to **Restorative Justice** participants in custody, providing some financial restoration through the work and certifications accomplished by those in-custody participants. Additionally, the State of Illinois aims to include the business, college, and farming communities throughout the state, along with mentors, retirees, and veterans, in receiving wages, tax breaks, subsidies, and grants. These groups will also be licensed to certify **Outside the Inside Restorative Justice** in-custody participants through the Illinois College Board.

Further, the State of Illinois intends to incorporate state surplus appropriations into every community to purchase abandoned lots and parcels in Illinois counties. This will allow for small homes built by participants to be placed on those properties, creating taxable income for the counties. This goal-oriented program is led by the community and aims to generate jobs, manufacturing opportunities, and educational initiatives that bring real solutions to reduce recidivism and the threat of crime. The program incorporates all branches of the community to create meaningful change.

Participants will receive minimum wages under a two-year agreement. Half of these wages will be distributed to victims of the crimes committed by the participant, or to the Illinois Victim Compensation Fund if no direct victims are named. One-quarter of the wages will be allocated to child support, court fees, fines, and public defender fees, which place a burden on counties throughout Illinois. The remaining quarter will be placed into a bank account, only to be distributed to the participants if they successfully complete the program. Upon completion, the sentencing judge will issue the funds along with a clerk-certified deed to a small home built by the participant.

Moreover, each participant will be certified in drug treatment, G.E.D. completion, welding, heating and air conditioning, and electrical repair and installation.

## More About RJOTIP

This program supports and embodies the old saying: **"It takes a village."** The point being that young citizens of this state need the opportunity, through guidance from our older citizens, to understand what it means to be a responsible member of society. This includes involvement from our businessmen and women, farmers, retirees, veterans, honorable judges, state attorneys, as well as representatives from the public defender's office and private practice attorneys. For the first time in ages, our community—made up of these individuals—will have a voice in a program in which they are literally invested through their tax dollars. Victims will no longer be just a topic of conversation; instead, they will receive some form of recourse and restoration through the work and accomplishments of the person who caused them harm in the first place.

This program is unlike anything the Illinois Department of Corrections has previously offered in terms of restorative justice. It is **hyper-focused** on restoration for the victims associated with defendants in the criminal justice system. Judges will decide whether a defendant is appropriate for this program, and whether the defendant has fully and unequivocally renounced any gang affiliations or activities. No participants involved in sex crimes or cases involving the taking of life will be allowed to participate. Only defendants charged with Class 3 or Class 4 felonies, through court-structured plea agreements, will be eligible for this opportunity. The elected judges, chosen by the citizens of our communities, will have the power—through your votes—to determine a defendant's eligibility to participate.

The **Restorative Justice Outside the Inside** program will be a community-based Illinois Department of Corrections facility, managed by IDOC employees, with the inclusion of business owners, retirees, veterans, and farmers. These individuals will be contracted and certified through the Illinois College Board to provide accreditation and certification in their respective fields of expertise. Certified instructors, alongside professors from local colleges, will serve as contractors within the program, teaching accepted participants life skills, anger management, conflict resolution, and "Morgue Impact Life" skills, which emphasize the value of being a citizen of our state. Participants will become certified in nine modules:

1. Welding
2. Heating and air conditioning
3. Building trades
4. Horticulture
5. Solar installation
6. Concrete maintenance and installation
7. Electrical engineering, repair, and installation
8. Basic drafting (architectural and mechanical)
9. Plumbing repair and installation

Additionally, participants will receive college accreditation for an **Associate of Applied Science (AAS)** degree, all within two years, while building prefabricated homes on-site at the community center, where up to 50 participants will live while attending the Rosecrance Drug, Alcohol, and Domestic Violence Treatment Program within the two-year structured period.

Participants in this program will work 50-hour weeks for minimum wages of $13.00 per hour. However, **three-quarters** of their wages will be waived over the two-year period. Of this:

- **Half of all wages** will be disseminated to victims, either directly or through the Illinois Victims Compensation Act Fund.
- **One quarter** of wages will go to Court Services and Child Support services for the program's duration.
- **The final quarter** will be saved in an account for the participant, to be awarded upon successful completion of the program.

With guidance from business owners, farmers, retirees, and veterans, participants will build prefabricated homes on-site. The State of Illinois will purchase abandoned lots or parcels, and, upon city code approval, the prefabricated homes will be placed on these lots. The homes will be built from the foundation up, including a garden or small acre of land, which will be deeded to the successful participant upon completion of the two-year program.

Currently, the Illinois Department of Corrections spends between $24,500 and $28,500 annually per person for care, custody, and control of each individual in custody. With federal grants related to solar installation and the Federal Rehabilitation Act Fund provided to the State of Illinois and the Illinois Department of Corrections, this program—including minimum wages and wages paid to retirees, veterans, business owners, farmers, instructors, and Rosecrance staff—will not cost Illinois taxpayers any more than it would if the participant were sent to one of the state's existing prisons.

While this program is available only to participants with Class 3 and Class 4 felonies, its structure and success could serve as a model for incorporating parts of the training into prison rehabilitation programs for higher-class felonies behind the walls and fences of other IDOC facilities.

This program is about **structure** and restoring not only the victims of crime but also the criminals to productive citizenship, as mandated by our Illinois Constitution. Taxpayers, as citizens, deserve the right to participate in a program that allows them to see their tax dollars change lives—for both victims and fellow citizens—by helping convicted felons become law-abiding Illinoisans. Participants will learn how to fill out voter registration cards, file taxes, pay taxes, and live as responsible citizens.

This program is for our communities, our state, and its people, forming a village that has a voice and a hands-on opportunity to affect us all as a community.

## Plea Agreement and Sentencing

The **Restorative Justice Outside the Inside** program of Illinois cannot be accessed through letters of recommendation or any other source except through a Circuit Court judge of Illinois and a plea agreement mutually agreed upon by the State's Attorney and the defendant's attorney.

This sentencing construct is only applicable to Class 3 and Class 4 felonies, with no admittance for sex offenders or murder cases. The sentencing tool is designed for judges to administer justice, prioritizing the victims above all. This sentencing must be taken seriously by the defendant and their attorney. If the defendant fails to meet all the criteria set forth in the contract, as well as the rules and regulations of the program, they will have violated the terms of the plea agreement. In such a case, the defendant will be returned to court before the same judge and will be sentenced in accordance with the statutes governing Class 3 or Class 4 felonies. The court will have the discretion to impose a sentence within the lower or upper range of the statutory guidelines, depending on the judge's determination of whether the defendant deserves a higher sentence.

This plea agreement is about **justice** for criminal acts that have harmed a person or persons within the community, their property, or their welfare. It aims to right those wrongs through a small semblance of restoration for the victims of the defendant's actions. The defendant submits to the program's primary objective: to restore them to productive citizenship, in line with the Illinois Constitution's requirements related to sentencing.

Under this program, the court will sentence the defendant to a full term of two years, without any allowance for good-time credits, as the program's modules, educational components, and behavioral modification programs (with accreditation for an Associate of Applied Science degree and vocational training) will require a full two years to complete. Additionally, the minimum wage earned by the defendant during these two years will be distributed as follows:

- **Half of all wages** will be awarded to the victims related to the defendant's case or deposited directly into the Victims Compensation Act Fund through the Secretary of the State of Illinois.

- **One-quarter of the wages** will be relinquished to Court Services and Child Support via DCFS, if applicable.

- **The final quarter** of the defendant's wages will be saved on their behalf, accruing interest. Upon successful completion of the program, a check will be awarded to the defendant, along with the keys to a small home they built, with a deed certified in the defendant's name for that property.

If the defendant is unsuccessful in the program, they will receive nothing except one-quarter of the wages earned.

This plea agreement represents a concerted effort involving community-based businesses, farmers, retirees, veterans, Rosecrance Domestic Battery and drug rehabilitation behavioral modification resources, the local morgue impact program, college instructors, and local unions, all of which contribute to the program. If the defendant fails, it will be entirely their fault—not that of the community, the court, or the state, which offers such an opportunity.

The plea agreement is designed by the legislature to affect the community and victims as a whole, providing justice for the victims while laying a foundation to ensure that the defendant never again commits offenses against another person, their property, or the law. This agreement will impact not only the victims of the crime but also the entire community if the defendant fails. In failing, the defendant will have chosen not to be restored to productive citizenship or to make amends for their criminal actions.

It is at the discretion of this court, and through the State of Illinois, that this plea agreement is made available. By signing the agreement, the defendant agrees to the terms of the contract and its enumerations for the **Restorative Justice Outside the Inside** program of Illinois. The terms are exact and will be voided based on the defendant's success or failure, it is entirely up to them.


## Restorative Justice Contract


**RESTORATIVE JUSTICE OUTSIDE THE INSIDE PROGRAM CONTRACT**
On behalf of the Outside the Inside Program of the State of Illinois

Upon acceptance of the plea agreement, I, *(print name)*, for a conviction for: _______ (a Class 3 or 4 Felony), in case number ___________ before the Honorable Judge ___________ , hereby, along with the plea agreement, accept the terms of that plea agreement and understand that I am waiving and allowing for the Good Time Statute application to be **not** earned or applied so that I may complete the Restorative Justice Outside the Inside Program of the State of Illinois for the purpose of module training, minimum wages earned and disseminated according to program guidelines, and accreditation for educational and behavioral modification modules, as well as the training required in accordance with certification for prefabrication of small home parts and installation therein. Upon completion, I will receive the placement and deed awarding of a small home, certification in nine modules, and thereafter, parole.

1. I also understand that I will serve a period of two calendar years between an Illinois Department of Corrections receiving and classification facility and placement in a Restorative Justice community center closest to this Court and the participating community center.
2. I also understand that wages paid to me (as required by minimum wage in the State of Illinois) will be withheld at a rate of 100%, and access to any funds related to total wages will not be allowed until or after successful completion of this program. Half of all wages will be immediately deducted and awarded to the Victims Compensation Act fund or disseminated directly to victims in the case in which I have been convicted. One quarter of all wages earned will be disseminated to Court Services and Child Support Services if applicable. In the event child support does not apply, Court Services will be awarded all wages up to and limited to one quarter of all wages. I agree to the award of one quarter of all wages earned at the end of the two-year completion of this program.

Attached are the particulars related to my understanding of what I agree to.

I, _____________, hereby agree to the terms of my plea agreement and to be restored to productive citizenship through every module required in this program. Behavior modification modules, as well as educational and vocational ones with the Morgue Impact program, are part of this agreement. By signing below before my attorney, I agree to follow the rules and regulations of the Illinois Department of Corrections and the rules of Rosecrance Drug and Domestic Battery inclusions, as well as the rules and regulations of this program enumerated herein. I understand that I will be ejected from this program if I violate the rules and regulations, or the particulars of my plea agreement related to this program. If I violate these rules and regulations, my wages will be forfeited and disseminated between the Victims or the Victims Compensation Act Fund, and Court Services or with "Child Support Services." I understand that if I violate the rules and regulations, I would also be waiving access to ownership and deed certification by the clerk of this court and clerk's office.

I swear under oath that I will follow all of the rules and regulations, and if I choose to violate any rules and regulations, I hereby waive any award earned within this program or enumerated certifications other than accumulated college credits. By signing below, I, _____________, hereby agree to these terms fully.

Defendant/Participant_______________________________
Defendant's Attorney _______________________________

## CONTRACT FOR PARTICIPANT/DEFENDANT

Upon acceptance of the plea agreement for a conviction of a Class 3 or Class 4 felony (or felonies) in the State of Illinois, the Defendant agrees to enter into the Restorative Justice Outside the Inside Program of Illinois on behalf of the Illinois Department of Corrections for a period of no less than two years. Good Time applications for normal sentences under this conviction do not apply in relation to acceptance of this plea under this contract to enter the program. However, they do apply under statute if the defendant/participant violates the program parameters or this contract's obligations and clauses. In such a case, the defendant would be subject to the maximum sentence or any sentence within the statutory range at the discretion of the sentencing judge in this case.

The construct of sentencing a Defendant/Participant to two full years without incorporating the Good Time construct is to allow and enforce the defendant to obtain all certifications and awards related to successfully completing the program and its criteria, as well as all program modules and program models that must be achieved and certified according to law, the Illinois College Board, the Illinois Department of Corrections, and Rosecrance Drug and Domestic Abuse Prevention Education Training.

By signing this contract in front of the sentencing judge and his or her attorney, the Participant/Defendant agrees to the plea agreement under statute, without Good Time, and according to the newly amended statute itemizing this program opportunity. This agreement proffering a sentence of two full years in the care, custody, and control of the Restorative Justice Outside the Inside Program of Illinois on behalf of the Illinois Department of Corrections.

The Defendant/Participant agrees to every articulation herein, and if any articulation in this contract is violated in any way, **THIS CONTRACT BECOMES VOID.** This means that the Defendant/Participant's behavior, acts, or inactions while in the program have violated this contract and the plea agreement attached to this contract in this specific case number and under this statute. The Defendant/Participant must then immediately be removed from the community site center and sent to the nearest County Jail or Justice Center holding facility, after which they will be returned to this Court for re-sentencing according to the Court's discretion under the statute.

If this Court determines that the allegations against the defendant are sufficient to re-sentence the defendant to a longer term than two years under the appropriate statute, the defendant under a new sentence will be credited for time already served under the Good Time guidelines set forth retroactively to the statute applied under the new sentence.

By affixing your signature alongside your attorney's signature, you, the defendant in this case, along with your lawyer, agree to the very strict and promising terms and clauses enumerated within your plea agreement and this contract, as follows and related herein:

1. I understand and agree that I am not involved in a gang. I am not, nor am I any longer, a participant in a gang or criminal enterprise.
2. I am no longer affiliated with any members of a gang. As such, if at any time after signing this contract, any official related to the IDOC or the Restorative Justice Outside the Inside Program—affiliates therein included, but not limited to, staff, officers, instructors, or representatives—witness any gang activity or gang signs represented or socializing or planning or anything construed as gang involvement will be immediate grounds for removal and by signing this, I understand fully.
3. Attached to this contract is my **Renunciation Oath**, which I have signed in front of my attorney. It itemizes the steps I took (if applicable) through my attorney and the Gang Crimes Unit of this county to ensure for the Court that I am not a member of any

organization, gang, or criminal enterprise. Alternatively, if I was a gang member, I would have gone through the process of renunciation and verification by the Gang Crimes Unit. They have reached out to my affiliated gang leadership, who are in charge of membership, and through counsel, they have demanded my release from membership. This release was authorized, approved, and verified by the Gang Crimes Unit to avoid prosecution under the R.I.C.O. Act if the gang hierarchy did not release me from its membership without retaliation. By signing this contract, I swear to this Court under oath and under penalty of perjury that I am not a gang member and that I will never in my life participate in one again. My **Oath of Renunciation** supports this clause. If at any time I violate this contract or my Oath of Renunciation, I understand and agree that this violation would be in breach of my plea agreement and this contract. By signing before my attorney and this Court, I understand and agree to this clause and the terms herein.

4. I also understand and agree that if, after successfully completing this program and being awarded a house deed with a minimum wage check, and at any time before my parole is served in its entirety, I commit a crime or participate in any gang activity verified by my parole officer, the house deed will be rescinded, and my parole will be violated. I will be resentenced as described in paragraph (1). By signing before my attorney and the Court, I, the Defendant/Participant, agree with the terms and clauses herein.

5. I agree and understand that as a Defendant/Participant entering the Restorative Justice Outside the Inside Program of Illinois, I am required to address and respond to all staff, officers, instructors, veterans, retirees, and all those in positions of authority within this program as "Ma'am" or "Sir." The construct is to show respect at all times to the staff within the program. "Yes, Sir," "No, Sir," "Yes, Ma'am," and "No, Ma'am" must be used. Failing to address staff or officers under this method of communication violates the rules and regulations of this program. I understand that I must address staff and all authority figures with respect and must use the "Yes, Sir", "No, Sir" construct for the entire two-year duration while in the program.  By signing before the Court with my attorney, I agree and understand the terms and requirements in this clause.

6. **(6)** By signing this contract, I also understand and agree as the defendant in this case and a new participant in the Restorative Justice Outside the Inside Program for Illinois to voluntarily relinquish three-fourths (3/4) of all of my wages for a fifty-hour workweek over two years, working ten hours a day, five days a week. This equates to wages at minimum wage ($13.00 per hour), of which three-fourths (3/4) of all wages earned each week will be relinquished for two years under the following methodology:
   - One half (1/2) of all wages will go to the victim(s) in this case for two years or to the Victims Compensation Act Fund of Illinois directly and weekly for two years as earned.
   - One quarter (1/4) of all wages will be given to Court Services for two years as earned, and one half (1/8) of that quarter will be relinquished for Child Support, if applicable.

No matter what is relinquished from my wages over the two-year period, three-fourths (3/4) of all wages must be paid to victims or to the Victims Compensation Act Fund and to Court Services in full. If applicable, Child Support will be paid to the mother of the defendant's children as verified by Child Services.

Finally, I agree to have one quarter (1/4) of all of my wages held in a secure account by the Illinois Treasurer or an appointed bank to accrue interest as applicable under basic interest rates and Illinois law. Upon successful completion of the program and the start of parole, the Court will award and certify the defendant/participant's deed to his or her home and property parcel or lot and provide the keys to said dwelling along with a check for the full amount of the defendant's earned wages for two years, with accrued interest, based on one quarter (1/4) of all wages earned.

I understand that by receiving only one quarter (1/4) of all wages earned, I agree to relinquish the other three-fourths (3/4) of all wages to the victims and/or the Victims Compensation Act Fund, and one quarter (1/4) to Court Services and/or Child Support if applicable. I understand and agree to the terms of this clause, and by signing along with my attorney, I verify this.

I also understand the need to restore my victims and the state in some way for the crime or crimes I have committed.

## Restorative Justice Rules and Regulations

1. All **Outside for the Inside Restorative Justice** participants will enter the program under a sentence or plea agreement by the sentencing judge within the jurisdiction of the Circuit Court for the county where the participant's crime occurred.

2. All participants must be verified as fully renounced from any gang or criminal enterprise.

3. All participants are required to enter the Illinois Department of Corrections under a sentence that allows them to serve not less than two full years, in order to acquire all module certifications and the benefits associated with building and relocating a small home on a lot or parcel purchased by the State of Illinois.

4. All participants are required to enter the Illinois Department of Corrections Receiving and Classification for the Southern, Central, or Northern Districts of Illinois, as required by the State of Illinois, to review the medical, mental, and educational needs of the participant. The participant will then be transferred to a community **Outside for the Inside Restorative Justice** site nearest to the participant's community in which they were sentenced.

5. All participants are required to refer to staff, officers, and instructors as "sir" or "ma'am" for the entire duration of the program.

6. All participants are required to acquire a G.E.D. and/or take a T.A.B.E. test to determine educational abilities before beginning Module One. If a participant has a high school diploma but scores less than an 8.0 on the T.A.B.E. test, they will be allowed to study and raise their scores to meet the above 8.0 requirement.

7. All participants must sign an agreement indicating their commitment to participate in the Rosecrance Peer Pressure Accountability Rehabilitation Program, which will be activated immediately upon the signing of the agreement. (Rules related to this program will be enumerated by Rosecrance staff/instructors).

8. All participants are required to participate in veteran-related issue groups led by veterans of all branches of service, including but not limited to the military, police, firefighters, nurses, doctors, and retirees from government roles.

9. At the discretion of instructors, staff, and mentors, participants will be required to visit city or county morgues to witness lives lost from within their community. Mentors and retirees from the police and gang crime units are encouraged to create instruction based on their experiences.

10. Participants will be required to authorize half of all minimum wages earned over the two-year duration in the program to be distributed to a victim compensation fund. This fund will pay each victim associated with the participant's crime(s) directly. If the participant has no individual victims named in their case, half of their wages must be allocated to the Illinois Victims Compensation Fund for victims of crime in Illinois. A quarter of all wages will be allocated for child support obligations (if any) and for payment of court costs, fines, and obligations. The final quarter of wages will be placed into a savings account to accrue interest on behalf of the participant. If the participant successfully completes the program, a check for the full amount will be issued to them, along with a deed certified by the clerk of the county court and keys to a small home.

11. All participants will be required to learn and master all module specifications and become certified in employable trades required for building and maintaining a small home and the property it is delivered to.

12. All participants must learn and master how to file taxes, register to vote, pay property taxes, and acquire property insurance (including flood, wind, and fire). They will also learn fire prevention, including the installation of smoke detectors, fire extinguishers, and other modern methods taught by instructors and insurance agents.

13. Each participant must be physically, educationally, and mentally able to handle the complexities of all learned modules related to building a small home and become certified in them. Additionally, they must be capable of dealing with the behavioral modification aspects of Rosecrance's criteria, Illinois Department of Corrections rules, and regulations, as well as other program requirements for a period of two consecutive years. Each participant must sign a contract agreeing to all rules and criteria. Any participant who does not sign the agreement is in violation of their sentencing agreement.

14. Each participant will be required to work no more than 10 hours per day under minimum wage criteria.

15. Each participant is required to attend all scheduled groups led by staff, veterans, retirees, or Rosecrance peer-pressure-led programming, including drug treatment and Psychology 101–404 programs. They will also attend lifestyle redirection, conflict resolution, anger management, morgue life impact programs, volunteering, and classes on organizational skills.

16. Each participant will be required to make crafts and cards during leisure time for family members for holidays or special occasions, as well as to volunteer to create these for needy families in the community, including but not limited to children's homes, domestic abuse shelters, nursing homes, and VFWs.

17. All participants will be required to:

a. Make their beds and keep their living quarters clean and neat.

b. Fold all clothing and keep all personal items and property organized and clean.

c. No participant may leave the group sleeping area until all areas are in full compliance with the cleanliness and organization requirements.

d. Participants are responsible as a team for the cleanliness and conduct of their group and for encouraging success through positive reinforcement and rewards based on Rosecrance criteria.

e. Participants are required to study for at least one hour per night without music or interruptions.

f. Participants are required to maintain good hygiene at all times.

g. Participants must engage in leisure activities quietly and respectfully, using headphones or earbuds when necessary.

h. Inappropriate sexual activity is prohibited. (See IDOC rules and regulations.)

i. Cursing and vulgar language are not permitted.

j. Phone calls must be made at reasonable times and must not conflict with scheduled work, school, or group activities.

k. Participants are required to engage in peer-led workouts, Monday through Friday at 5:00 a.m., for 20–30 minutes.

l. Participants are allowed to email and access their tablets during breaks, or as reasonably permitted throughout the day and night.

m. Participants must follow all rules and orders with a respectful and courteous attitude.

n. Participants must wash, dry, and iron their individual clothing and state-issued items.

o. Participants are required to master the use of safety gear, including clothing and masks.

p. Participants must help maintain the Restorative Justice community center by keeping it clean and engaging in beautification activities, such as landscaping, planting trees, raking leaves, mowing lawns, and de-icing walkways.

q. Participants will be required to shave and receive weekly haircuts, with payment for haircuts provided by the inmate benefit fund.

r. Participants may order commissary items through vendors approved by IDOC and Community Restorative Justice administrators.

s. Visits will take place in person or by video on weekends between 8:00 a.m. and 8:00 p.m., with a limit of four hours per visit and up to eight in-person visits per month. Weekday visits are between 5:30 p.m. and 8:30 p.m. Video visits are limited to one per week. Participants are responsible for ensuring visits do not interfere with any program obligations.

t. Participants will work in groups of three to cook, clean, attend groups, and engage in group activities. They must support each other in accountability and positive peer relationships that foster trust, friendship, and citizenship.

u. Participants may send and receive money on their trust fund accounts within the community center.

v. Participants may attend religious services under IDOC rules and regulations.

w. Participants with dietary or religious needs will be accommodated according to IDOC rules.

x. Participants requiring medications will be provided with necessary prescriptions per IDOC rules and medical guidelines.

y. ADA accommodations will be provided as required by Illinois statutes to ensure a safe working environment.

## Day in the Life
### Weekday Schedule

**5:00 a.m.** – Wake-up call for all participants.
**5:15 a.m.** – All participants are required to make their beds, clean their area, wash, brush their teeth, and get into their Class-A uniform before breakfast.
**5:45 a.m.** – All participants must be seated in their respective dining areas. Participants working in the dining and kitchen areas will serve breakfast by a dish-and-pass method to all participants.
**6:00 a.m.** – Breakfast is over. All participants are required to clean their dining areas together and ensure all dishes and utensils are placed into bins for those assigned to the kitchen to clean and dry.
**6:05 a.m.** – All participants are given 55 minutes to send emails, make phone calls, or engage

in personal tasks, such as studying or writing in their journals. (No games are allowed at this time.)

**7:00 a.m.** – Count time. All participants must sit on the end of their beds in Class-A uniforms, ensuring their areas are in compliance with IDOC rules and regulations.

**7:10 a.m. – 7:15 a.m.** – IDOC employees will dismiss participants at their discretion once the count is secured and all participants are in compliance.

**7:15 a.m.** – Exercise begins for all participants, lasting for 30 minutes. Exercise can be group-based or led by a designated participant. This is required five days a week, and all participants must take part. Accommodations will be made for handicapped participants as needed.

**7:45 a.m.** – Participants have 15 minutes to shower, dress, and bring their areas back into compliance before school/programs begin.

**8:00 a.m.** – All participants assigned to behavioral modification programs or educational modules must sign out with an IDOC employee. Participants taking medication will be administered medication by a nurse at this time. Any participants with doctor's appointments or sick call are excused.

**8:05 a.m.** – All participants must be at their assigned modules. No module may have more than five participants at a time. This includes behavioral, educational, and vocational modules, which operate on a rotational basis.

**8:05 a.m. – 12:30 p.m.** – Participants must ensure that all module materials are safely stored before lunch. No materials are allowed to be removed from the module site to the dining areas.

**12:30 p.m. – 12:45 p.m.** – Lunch is served in the dining room under the same rules and procedures as breakfast.

**12:50 p.m.** – All participants must return to their respective module sites.

**2:55 p.m.** – Count time. All participants must freeze and allow IDOC employees to count them. This procedure ends when IDOC staff verbally dismisses the participants.

**5:30 p.m.** – All participants must ensure that all safety and assigned tools are returned and that their module areas are clean.

**5:35 p.m.** – Participants are required to go directly to the dining area for dinner.

**5:50 p.m.** – After dinner, participants must return to their living quarters for personal activities such as washing, cleaning, showering, playing games, making phone calls, or other leisure activities.

**7:30 p.m.** – All participants must attend night modules for study, tutoring, or behavioral modification programming.

**8:45 p.m.** – Participants must return to their living quarters and be respectful and quiet, allowing others to prepare for bedtime, study, or make phone calls or emails.

**9:30 p.m.** – Lights out. Count time. All participants must be at their bed sites, dressed appropriately for the count, either in bedtime attire or pajamas.

**9:35 p.m.** – No talking, games, phone calls, or emails. Lights out, and rest must follow in preparation for the next day's work.

*Participants working in dietary positions will rotate monthly with other participants to learn culinary skills related to cooking, cleaning, and food preparation.*

**Weekend Schedule**

**5:00 a.m.** – Wake-up call for all participants.
**5:15 a.m.** – All participants are required to make their beds and clean their living spaces.
**5:45 a.m.** – Participants are allowed to go to breakfast.
**6:00 a.m. – 7:00 a.m.** – Participants must clean all areas of the community center where they work, study, eat, work out, and engage in leisure activities.
**7:00 a.m.** – Count time. All participants must be seated on their beds until dismissed by IDOC employees.
**7:15 a.m.** – Once count is cleared, participants are allowed to move freely within the community center to designated areas for leisure activities, visits with family and friends, emails, phone or video visits, and commissary access.
**12:30 p.m.** – Lunch time.
**12:45 p.m.** – Participants must check in for scheduled drug counseling, behavioral modification programs, domestic abuse prevention sessions, etc. Each participant must attend and complete at least one module during this time until all accreditations related to these programs are acquired.
**2:55 p.m.** – Count time. All participants must be in their living spaces, seated on their beds, until dismissed by IDOC employees.
**3:05 p.m.** – Participants may return to leisure activities, visiting, or phone calls.
**5:50 p.m.** – Dinner. Afterward, participants may return to leisure activities until 7:30 p.m.
**7:30 p.m.** – Participants must write in their journals for impact programs related to topics such as death, life, victims, and behaviors, or engage in study. Verification must be shown to retirees and veterans.
**8:45 p.m.** – Participants must return to their living spaces and prepare for bed. They may make phone calls or send emails as long as they are quiet and respectful.
**9:30 p.m.** – Count time. All participants must be in their beds for the count until dismissed by IDOC employees.
**10:00 p.m.** – Lights out. Bedtime.


## Community Center Sites


Community center sites throughout Illinois should be similar to work release centers, with the key distinction that **Restorative Justice Center** participants are not allowed to leave the center except for supervised construction work on approved building sites (e.g., city lots or parcels of land). Community sites must not exceed a 50-bed capacity and must house all participants for the full duration of their two-year sentence, which includes the completion of the small homes' fabrication and their assembly at appointed home sites.


The center itself must be built to accommodate housing for all participants, providing meals for those in custody, along with a gymnasium for exercise and workouts. There must be enough classrooms to facilitate behavioral modification modules and a religious chapel to support participants' right to practice their religion. The center must also provide sufficient space to accommodate **Rosecrance** staff, as well as any behavioral modification, drug rehabilitation, or domestic battery prevention training needed by each participant and staff trainee.

Additionally, the community center must include a kitchen and dining room to accommodate staff, IDOC employees, retirees, veterans, professors, college instructors, and business and farmer instructors. A separate dining area is to be provided for **Restorative Justice** participants. All community Restorative Justice Centers are the property of the Illinois Department of Corrections (IDOC) and will be constructed according to the code and security requirements mandated by the Illinois Department of Corrections throughout the state. Community sites will include bathrooms for participants, staff, and security personnel, with separate facilities for each group. Janitorial duties for the entire community center will be assigned to participants.

Each community center will feature an administrative building with offices for counselors, security, and staff responsible for performing administrative duties, similar to any other IDOC facility. Community centers will also operate an in-custody commissary for staff and participants (subject to IDOC approval). Each center will establish a trust fund or business office to hold and disburse funds on behalf of the in-custody participants.

The centers must also include areas for in-custody visitation and a **Family Reunification Center**, where participants can engage with their children through activities such as drawing, coloring, video games, and other planned events to help reunify families. Concessions and food purchases will be available via debit cards purchased in accordance with IDOC standards and approval. A program called **"Freshly Favorites"** will allow vendors from the public and community to sell food to in-custody participants weekly.

Every community center must have space to build **seven small homes** (27' x 27' feet) at any given time, along with the ability to store materials and break them down for transport via "sally ports" that are large enough to accommodate the loading and unloading of small home materials. The **Restorative Justice Outside the Inside** program will have a warden or Chief Operating Officer and will be structured like any other IDOC facility in terms of employee duties and responsibilities.

Community center sites must be secure on all sides and will require IDOC staff to patrol both the perimeter and interior of the center. Although part of a restorative justice program, these centers will still be considered IDOC facilities and must remain secure at all times for the safety of the community, staff, and participants within the program. The community center must be built by outside contractors approved by IDOC in Springfield and by the city in which the community center is located. These must be unionized contractors who are awarded bids to complete each center.

Whenever possible, community members must be allowed to participate in public meetings regarding the location of the community center and any other concerns the public may have before approval or disapproval of the site(s).

For all purposes described here, the community sites mentioned are state facilities, owned and operated by IDOC employees, contracted members, and staff enumerated within the program.

## Rosecrance

Rosecrance is an established treatment facility located in Winnebago County, Rockford, Illinois. It plays a vital role in the rehabilitation and restoration of victims of domestic battery and drug abuse. Often, offenders are also victims of habitual drug addiction and, in many cases, were once victims of domestic abuse within their own families. Rosecrance is crucial as a "treatment module" for addressing drug abuse and implementing prevention methods related to domestic violence. Behavioral modification programming is essential for transforming "criminal thinkers" and idle minds that are untrained in productive citizenship.

Kurtis M. Williams, once a juvenile, attended the Durand campus of Rosecrance, where he was trained in peer-pressure behavioral modification techniques. The inclusion of intensive techniques through behavioral modification during the two-year program is crucial. These techniques help ensure that cause-and-effect modifications are embedded within the broader framework of the Restorative Justice program, which aims for rehabilitation and restoration.

Currently, Illinois faces widespread issues with domestic violence, drug abuse, and overdose deaths throughout its communities. Veterans, retirees, and IDOC employees, along with Rosecrance instructors and therapists, are essential to the success of this program. As such, the authors invite Rosecrance, along with its curriculum, instructors, and staff, to be part of this initiative. Their involvement is essential for meeting the behavioral modification needs and supporting the proposed accredited Psychology 101-404 educational modules.

## Victims Restoration

This program differs from most proposed ideas in that victims are rarely, if ever, included in the benefits of any programs. They are, in fact, victims of crime, whether it be through physical harm, property loss, or the trauma related to such incidents. The justice system is intended to balance that equation. However, **punishment without restoration** does little to help victims heal. In cases of major crimes such as murder, rape, armed robbery, carjacking, or child sexual assault, the trauma often never leaves. Punishment for the perpetrators should be swift and exact, and the criminal justice system ensures this. However, this program is not designed to provide murderers and rapists with an easy way out. There are separate programs within the Illinois Department of Corrections for those in-custody offenders.

This program is open only to Class 3 and Class 4 felony offenders through plea agreements approved by circuit court judges within the participating judicial circuits and counties where the program is funded. It offers **some level of restoration** for victims by providing half of all wages earned over two years (at $13.00 per hour for 50 hours per week), with no taxes withheld. These funds will either go directly to the specific victims of the defendant's crimes or to the

Illinois Victims Compensation Act Fund. Illinois is a state that cares about its citizens, and when they are victimized by crime, this state is taking steps to restore some faith in its justice system through programs like this.

When we, as a state, create programs that include victims of crime while also restoring criminals to productive citizenship through highly structured programming, modules, and behavioral modification with certifications and home ownership, we involve the community—business owners, college instructors, teachers, veterans, retirees, and farmers. In doing so, we become hands-on participants in the betterment of the judicial process and its goal of justice through restoration. We are not pampering criminals or their crimes. We are offering an opportunity for **hard work and change** in a manner that will not be easy for any participant. These offenders may enter the program with twisted criminal mindsets, but they will leave as productive, restored citizens.

## Veterans and Their Responsibilities

**Mission Statement Regarding Veterans:** The **Restorative Justice Outside the Inside** program will make reasonable efforts to reach out within Illinois communities to provide employment, training, and mentorship opportunities for veterans in **Restorative Justice Community Corrections Centers** throughout the state.

1. Employment must be full-time, with a wage of no less than $20.00 per hour, and must include full benefits, including but not limited to medical and dental coverage.

2. Responsibilities include, but are not limited to:

   - Training and orienting IDOC participants in ethics, tax and voting registration, and organizational skills related to personal finances and responsibilities such as managing a checkbook, paying bills, and maintaining a home.

   - Teaching respectful behavior, including addressing authority figures with "yes, sir," "no, sir," "yes, ma'am," and "no, ma'am."

3. Veterans are responsible for ensuring that participants wake up at 5:30 a.m., maintain personal hygiene, keep their quarters clean, eat, and exercise in formation, and prepare for the day's scheduled events and goals.

4. Veterans must counsel and encourage participants, acting as intermediaries between participants, officers, instructors, and the curriculum being taught.

5. Veterans must ensure that participants respectfully recite the **Pledge of Allegiance** each workday.

6. Veterans are required to hold participants accountable to the **Rosecrance** curriculum, specifically regarding peer pressure, drug treatment, and behavioral transitions.

7. Veterans employed by the program are also considered IDOC employees and must familiarize themselves with IDOC rules and regulations. They are required to report violations of rules and write **Disciplinary Reports** (DR-504) for IDOC violations.

## Retirees' Responsibilities

**Retirees** of this program include former police officers, first responders such as ambulance technicians, paramedics, firefighters, correctional officers, teachers, and jail staff. These individuals have spent their lives relating to people and meeting their needs. Retirees do not need extensive retraining; they need to understand the program's specific goals and the requirements of the modules and behavioral modification programs in which they will participate. Retirees are employees of the **Restorative Justice Outside the Inside** program and the Illinois Department of Corrections. Their duties and responsibilities include:

1. Supporting all functions, staff, and employees of the Illinois Department of Corrections for the two-year duration of the program.

2. Understanding that their employment is for a two-year term, and that other retirees will have the opportunity for employment during the next term.

3. Retirees are not part of any unions, unlike IDOC staff and employees. However, they will receive benefits such as dental coverage, full healthcare, and wages of no less than $20.00 per hour, with eight-hour shifts.

4. The purpose of employing retirees is not just to promote respect and traditional values in adherence to the program's rules and regulations, but also because retirees bring a wealth of life experience in dealing with people and hard-pressed situations. Their involvement is crucial to the success of this program, as they will guide participants through trials and hard work to become productive citizens.

5. Retirees will enter all living spaces and have the authority to enforce compliance with all rules and regulations of the program. They will study and understand the rules of the Illinois Department of Corrections and this program and will be responsible for writing disciplinary tickets when necessary. They will participate in every program module, alongside veterans.

6. Retirees will freely interact with participants in their studies and throughout the community center. They will hold participants accountable for their actions, ensuring that they follow the program's rules and meet its goals. The primary objective is to teach participants how to become responsible citizens and workers, certified in nine modules, with the skills to own and maintain homes and live as law-abiding Illinoisans.

# RESTORATIVE JUSTICE: OUTSIDE THE INSIDE OF THE STATE OF ILLINOIS PART 2

Kurtis M. Williams

## More About RJOTIP, Part 2

RESTORATIVE JUSTICE OUTSIDE THE INSIDE PROGRAM
A Lifer's Perspective on Restorative Justice
By Kurtis M. Williams
May2021

I saw on the local news, Channel 6, that the Illinois legislature is proposing a bill to offer grants to inmates being released, in the amount of $7,000 or more. I wasn't privy to the house bill number, and if they mentioned it, I was too shocked by the proposal to remember. This idea is extraordinary! If applied properly, it could literally change the foundation of justice reform for inmates, encouraging meaningful change with real substance.

In Illinois, the concept of restorative justice is a predicate for failure if it does not address the individuals connected to criminal enterprises and organizations tied to communities and inmates. Currently, the state of Illinois spends approximately $18,000 to $24,000 annually to incarcerate each of the 38,000 inmates in custody. It is my understanding that the Illinois legislature has proposed the possibility of offering grants between $7,000 and $10,000 to help inmates "get on their feet" after release, with the hope of encouraging employment opportunities and CDL certifications. This is an outstanding opportunity. However, without the involvement of every justice entity—judges, prosecutors, public defenders, and community employers—this initiative will lack the strength to not only support inmates' success but also ensure the safety and security of society at large.

Currently, in our criminal justice system, state's attorneys offer plea agreements to pretrial detainees as a way to save taxpayers the expense of jury trials and to provide defendants with an opportunity for a lesser sentence. If the legislature offers grants to inmates to "get on their feet after release," then it should consider requiring that a defendant earn that opportunity.

First and foremost, the state and public should be assured that plea agreements are not extended to gang members or individuals tied to criminal enterprises who could be violators under the RICO Act. Renunciation from such enterprises should be mandatory before any plea agreements are offered. Courts and the state should ensure that any plea agreements tied to restorative justice benefits first require a public renunciation from the defendant, verified through techniques approved by the gang crimes unit in the respective counties of Illinois. Any violations or evidence of continued ties to such organizations should void any access to the benefits offered in these agreements.

Moreover, before any plea agreements for restorative justice are accepted, the defendant should be required to relinquish any weapons that could harm others in the community. It's essential that guns be removed from the reach of defendants who are committing to restorative justice. The state and county, through tax incentives or corporate contracts, should offer incentives like a new pair of shoes (e.g., Nikes) in exchange for turning in weapons. This quid pro quo arrangement would allow defendants to be rewarded for "giving up the tools" without facing criminal arrest for possession—unless, of course, the weapons are tied to a murder, which should be clearly communicated upfront.

Additionally, the Illinois Department of Corrections should require trainee correctional officers to attend plea hearings involving restorative justice agreements. This would help them understand the intent and details of the agreements, which would directly impact their duties within the correctional facility. By being present in court, correctional officers will be better equipped to hold offenders accountable for their commitments and encourage their success in the program.

## Program Implementation

IDOC should assure the state and courts that all defendants under restorative justice plea agreements are sent to facilities closer to the communities where they will be paroled. This allows employers with "bonding" contracts to access former inmates for employment, improving their chances for reintegration. The Illinois Department of Corrections should also partner with companies like Tru-Built and other contractors to provide inmates with access to small home ownership (12'x12' homes) at a rate of $4,500 per home, on one acre of land. The logic is simple: if you require someone to live in a 10' x 10' cell for years and then expect them to succeed upon release, it will be too difficult. Such a program would establish credit, permanence, character, and self-esteem for the parolee.

Programs like anger management, conflict resolution, drug treatment, GED attainment, and job certification must be required. Employers should have access to prisons to train prospective employees and provide certification materials. For instance, CDL test materials are already available to inmates through their Inspire 2.0 tablets. These tablets should be used to access a wide range of employment materials. Without job prospects, how can a parolee repay the grants with their taxes and contribute to society?

Restorative justice cannot simply be a gift from the state—it must require a commitment from offenders to give up their old lives, thinking, and ties to the criminal lifestyle. The state, through its courts and IDOC, must ensure that the public knows this prospective restorative justice member is reformed and capable of success.

I'm sure you can appreciate the opportunities this restorative justice initiative could create if implemented. It offers prospects for employers, developers, real estate agents, surveyors, circuit clerks, and therapists specializing in drug treatment, anger management, and conflict resolution. It also has the potential to remove weapons from our streets, eliminate criminal organizations that plague our communities, and instill self-esteem and character in former offenders. While not all will succeed, I am confident that if opportunity is paired with hope and real direction, many offenders would choose this path over their current life choices.

I wish I could sit down with you, the U.S. Attorney, and Illinois representatives. I know where the cancer in our communities thrives. This restorative justice plan, combined with the RICO Act under federal law, could eliminate most gangs and the addictions they foster through illegal drugs and weapons. By targeting their property and homes, we could force them to turn in their members to protect their assets. Based on their loyalty to greed and criminal thinking, this would work.

Thank you for listening and reading. As always, be safe, and let me know what you think!

## BUSINESS OWNERS' INCLUSION AND RESPONSIBILITIES

No other rehabilitative program in Illinois relies as heavily on business owners. Often, business owners are victims of crime themselves, and with insurance premiums so high, they struggle to make ends meet. This program cannot run without business owners serving as instructors, who are certified through the Illinois College Board to train and certify inmate participants, enabling them to become productive, certified citizens in their respective fields of expertise.

Business owners who are plumbers, heating and air conditioning specialists, welding experts, concrete professionals, building trades specialists, draftsmen and women, electricians, horticulture experts, solar installation and green energy specialists, carpenters, and union members will all be inclusively certified through the Illinois College Board. They will help train participants to become experts who will build their own prefabricated small homes while earning wages to repay both their victims and the system in which they were convicted.

For the first time, external business owners, veterans, retirees, and farmers will run the program. This initiative will also include drug counseling through Rosecrance, inclusionary programming, and domestic violence prevention methods, with "Morgue Impact" training integrated as a community approach. All of this ensures that Illinois' constitutional guarantee to restore offenders to productive citizenship is fulfilled without any additional cost to taxpayers.

## FARMERS INCLUSION AND RESPONSIBILITIES

Farmers, who are pillars of our community and economy, deserve a seasonal opportunity to earn wages and benefits for their families while also becoming Illinois College Board-certified to train others in their respective fields of expertise. Farmers will be allowed to submit bids and ideas related to curriculum that encompasses the vocational expertise of horticulture, training participants in this field. This training will focus on the relationship between horticulture and farming, including the use of raised gardens for fruit bushes and trees suitable for small home sites, as well as its application to larger homes, businesses, and farms.

Farmers will provide participants with hands-on, seasonal vocational training, aligned with the farmers' availability to participate in the program. This module will prioritize the seasonal availability of the instructor/farmer and will be supplemented by veterans and retirees who will assist with the curriculum and training. The goal is not only for every participant to become certified in the vocational trade of horticulture, but also to gain practical experience in raised gardening, greenhouse construction, and essential survival techniques. This includes managing small ponds for raising tilapia and other edible foods, harvesting eggs, and raising chickens, among other skills.

Farmers are the backbone of our society and communities and must be accommodated in this program to help meet green-energy goals, support sustainable food growth, and promote the safe use of land, as small homeowners learn the vital skills of the farming trade.

## ILLINOIS COLLEGE BOARD CERTIFICATIONS

By signing legislation into law, the Governor of the State of Illinois will approve and activate the Restorative Justice Outside the Inside Program for the state. This activation authorizes the "certification" of each module taught by farmers, retirees, veterans, morgue technicians and coroners, teachers, business owners, and Rosecrance behavioral modification specialists. The program covers conflict resolution, anger management, and other behavioral impact programs, including domestic violence impact sciences. All certifications under this program will be contracted and accredited through the Illinois College Board, aligned with the Associate of Applied Science degree criteria and vocational sciences within building trades certifications. Participants must complete their GED requirements, if applicable, before completing the program, and will earn 68 college credits toward an Associate of Applied Science degree, along with specific certifications for each vocational module.

The Illinois College Board will be responsible for ensuring that every instructor, including farmers, morgue technicians, coroners, teachers, veterans, retirees, business owners, and behavioral modification specialists, is "certified" to teach in their respective fields. These criteria and certifications will align with the suggested curriculum attached, and may also include additional contributions from business owners, veterans, farmers, retirees, or other educational entities within the program. These certifications do not alter existing accreditations but add value to previously overlooked areas.

Anger management, conflict resolution, lifestyle redirection, and other behavioral sciences will be covered by existing Psychology 101–404 curriculum and taught by college instructors contracted for the program, alongside veterans, retirees, morgue technicians, and others. The goal is to achieve full "accreditation" in behavioral restoration.

Vocational training already in place—such as welding, plumbing, solar installation and maintenance, horticulture, cement installation and maintenance, heating and air conditioning, electrical work, carpentry, architectural and mechanical drafting, and building trades—will be taught by contracted business owners and farmers. Veterans and retirees will also play a role in delivering this vocational training. The ultimate goal is to train and certify participants in both vocational and behavioral skills, as well as provide education that will enable them to build a small home and start a new life as restored, productive citizens.

The expertise of the Illinois College Board will be essential to achieving these goals, and their involvement must be secured through a contract that minimizes delays or bureaucratic obstacles to ensure swift and efficient implementation for the people of Illinois.

## CITIZENS AND THEIR RESPONSIBILITIES

Citizens of Illinois have the responsibility to ensure that this program becomes a reality within their respective communities. Currently, Class Three and Four offenders are recidivating at a rate of 99%, costing between $24,000 to $28,000 per year without access to certified or accredited programming. These offenders are re-offending with only $10 in their pockets when they leave one of the 28 prisons throughout Illinois. This program will stop the re-offending process immediately! It puts judges back in control of their courtrooms and provides state attorneys with a tool, at the judge's discretion, to plea-bargain offenders into a program that benefits victims of crime, business owners, farmers, retirees, veterans, as well as court services and recipients of child support. Rosecrance's inclusionary programming will help restore the community by rehabilitating offenders and preparing them to re-enter society as productive citizens. This rehabilitation includes training, certification, and ultimately, small home ownership. Offenders will complete nine modules to earn certification, transforming them into taxpayers who now have something to lose.

Citizens must hold their politicians accountable for the use of their tax dollars. This program costs taxpayers no more than what would be spent on two years of imprisonment without reducing recidivism, while also transforming the criminal thinker into a productive, taxpaying citizen. Victims will receive the wages earned by the defendant participant for two years. Court services and child support services will also receive all wages earned by the defendant participant during this period. If the participant is successful, he or she will build and own a small home, become certified in nine fields of expertise, and retain the last of their earned wages. This program, called *Restorative Justice Outside the Inside of Illinois*, demonstrates that it takes a village to raise a citizen. You, John and Jane Citizen, hold your politicians accountable by working inclusively through veterans, retirees, business owners, farmers, and union members.

## GRADUATION AND CERTIFICATIONS AND AWARDS

Graduation from this program requires the Illinois College Board to award each participant an Associate of Applied Science degree. These degrees will either include all the vocational modules completed by the participant or, alternatively, the Illinois College Board will issue nine individual certifications for expertise in each respective field trained and certified within the two-year program.

Each participant must receive full certification in their respective fields of expertise. These certifications must be signed by the project superintendent, the relevant business owner, farmers (where applicable), college instructors, the dean of the participating college, and a representative from the Illinois College Board. In addition to their certifications, participants will receive a certified deed to their property and small home, along with the keys and codes to their security systems. At the graduation ceremony, participants will be honored by a circuit court judge, the State's Attorney, and their invited families.

Retirees, veterans, business owners, instructors, and farmers who participated in the program are invited to attend both the graduation ceremony and the celebratory reception. Following the ceremony, participants will be processed according to IDOC policies and procedures and allowed to leave the community site upon completion of this process.

New participants, staff, business owners, retirees, and farmers will be selected for the next two-year program through a bidding and lottery system. For the first 30 days of the new cycle, the outgoing administration will train the incoming members to ensure a smooth transition. During this period, former trainees will receive an additional 30 days of pay to assist the new members in adjusting to their responsibilities.

Graduation marks a significant achievement and offers an opportunity for the community to come together in celebration of the participants' success. It is also a time to reflect on the positive impact the program has had, including the restoration of victims, as a result of its inclusion in the community.

## APPROPRIATIONS AND GRANTS FOR THE COSTS OF THIS PROGRAM

The costs associated with onsite building needs and construction are covered by the United States Infrastructure Bill, passed and signed into law by President Biden in 2023. The United States Infrastructure Act specifically provides rehabilitative funds to Illinois for projects and programs such as this. The inclusion of solar installation and maintenance training, small home prefabrication, horticulture, and the latest heating and space-saving techniques are all covered by grants and appropriations within the 2023 Infrastructure Bill.

While appropriations are awarded through the Illinois Governor and legislature, the $24,500 allocated annually for housing an inmate in the Illinois Department of Corrections is a key consideration. The expenses related to this program will not cost Illinois taxpayers any more than what is already being paid annually to house inmates. Additionally, the inclusion costs for materials and minimum wages earned over the two-year program duration are covered by the United States Rehabilitation Act. This Act, along with the Infrastructure Bill, also covers wages and labor for the purposes of rehabilitation.

The authors of this program wish to clarify that labor unions are encouraged to participate in the construction of these centers through the standard bidding processes. We are not excluding union labor; on the contrary, we welcome union involvement. We simply ask that those responsible for facilitating the adoption of this program be allowed to research and verify that the cost representations made herein are accurate and in line with the outlined funding sources.

**ADDITIONAL DETAILS ON THE CONTENTS AND CURRICULUM OF THE PROGRAM**

## RE-ENTRY SIMULATOR INCLUSION

Re-entry simulators are already available through a program called *Just Income* by Community Spring, which is led by formerly incarcerated individuals. The re-entry simulator is especially important for teaching and training offenders in relation to their release. It helps in-custody offenders learn how to make decisions based on scheduled priorities, rather than on-the-fly choices. The simulator presents a variety of no-win dilemmas that people on parole or probation have to navigate on a regular basis. For example, in one scenario, the newly released offender must decide which presents a bigger risk: missing an appointment with a parole officer or missing work.

In *Reentry*, you have seven minutes to navigate life on parole or probation while adhering to the terms of your release. Unfortunately, three violations of your probation or parole conditions will send you back to prison. These non-criminal or "technical" violations are a significant driver of incarceration for people on parole or probation. In fact, supervision violations account for 42% of prison admissions nationwide. The *Outside the Inside* program should adopt simulator technologies like this to prepare all participants for life after incarceration.

The program operates as follows: You start the simulator with $60 in your pocket and instructions to meet with your parole or probation officer at regular intervals. However, within seconds of starting, the simulator asks you to "spin the wheel," which presents difficult decisions and circumstances beyond your control—many of which pose imminent threats to your freedom. Your $60 disappears quickly as fees and everyday costs begin to pile up. The simulator demonstrates how, in many states, a single monthly probation fee can consume your entire $60, and you'll be hit with a violation if you can't pay. What happens if a traffic accident blocks the road when you're on your way to meet your parole officer, or if you miss a curfew, an appointment, or work? Do you spend your last few dollars on an ID card or try to get by without one?

Do you take your friend's under-the-table job offer to make the money you desperately need, or turn it down to avoid being punished for unreported income? These scenarios demonstrate the contradictory nature of re-entry and highlight the artificial roadblocks faced by those simply trying to get their lives back on track. At the same time, the simulator creates a conflicting environment, forcing participants to make choices related (or not) to their restoration as productive citizens. Citizens of Illinois and our nation face similar choices every day without committing crimes to avoid their responsibilities.

Soon, it's time for your appointment with the parole officer. They're running late, but you can't afford to be late for work. Do you wait for the meeting or leave for work? As the simulator continues, it becomes clear that it is not designed to allow you to succeed easily, but to challenge you with real-life scenarios that re-entry offenders commonly face.

The inclusion of such a program would be highly beneficial. The simulator could be used for conflict resolution, anger management, and as part of a psychology curriculum (Psychology 101-404) to test participants both at the beginning of the program and prior to graduation. Modern technology is familiar to offenders, so the simulator would be a relevant and valuable upgrade for this program. It should also be considered for inclusion in re-entry programs within Illinois Department of Corrections (IDOC) facilities.

## CONFLICT RESOLUTION UNDER THE ACCREDITATION OF PSYCHOLOGY

Levels:101 through 404

**Conflict Resolution: What Is It?**

The instructor/professor begins by discussing with each individual in custody their understanding of conflict resolution. Participants must provide written examples of their understanding, perceptions, and triggers. Each student/participant is required to date and sign their responses.

**Definition of Conflict:** Conflict arises when opposites disagree or when opinions clash, creating controversy. Conflicts may be "actual," "potential," or "implied."

- **Actual conflict** occurs when a controversy exists between one or more persons.
- **Potential conflict** refers to situations where conflicting interests may develop but have not yet occurred. This creates a stressful period, often accompanied by fear of the unknown, which can lead to anger.

**Psychology Defined:** Psychology is the scientific study of the behavior of organisms, including human beings. Understanding ourselves is an ongoing, daily process—through our thoughts, verbal responses, body language, and the decisions we make, such as drawing "lines in the sand." These "lines" are the limitations we impose on what we are willing to accept and what we refuse to tolerate. For example:

- "If someone calls me a name, I'm going to fight."
- "If you insult my family, it's on."

These responses are often premeditated, leaving little room for reasoning or considering circumstances.

**Reason and Responsibility:** No one, under any circumstances, has the right to hurt another person. There are no justifications for planning to harm others, forcing them to accept our views, or intimidate them. A reasonable person defends themselves or their family only when faced with life-threatening or imminent harm. A criminal thinker, on the other hand, excuses violence.

**Criminal Thinkers:** Criminal thinkers are those with low impulse control, often shaped by early peer influence and inconsistent or abusive discipline. Their responses to stimuli are based on immaturity and poor training. Not all criminal thinkers commit crimes, but their negative responses to conflict can escalate anger, leading to violence. Without skills to manage these reactions, conflicts often spiral into harmful outcomes.

**Example: The White Rhinos in Africa** In the Serengeti Game Reserve, white rhinos were being killed, but not by poachers. Game wardens discovered through surveillance footage that juvenile elephants, left without mature leadership, were killing the rhinos for "fun." The juveniles lacked the guidance of a matriarch or a dominant male elephant to teach them. Once the wardens reintroduced adult elephants into the herd, the juveniles' destructive behavior stopped.

This example demonstrates how, like juvenile elephants, individuals without proper guidance can act out in harmful ways. The introduction of experienced adults helped curb the destructive impulses of the young elephants.

## Responses

In the same way adult elephants intervened to correct the juveniles' behavior, adults can intervene in human conflicts to prevent escalation. Discuss how the presence of mature individuals changed the behavior of the juvenile elephants and relate this to human conflict resolution.

- **Key Discussion:** How did the adult elephants stop the juveniles from acting out, and what can we learn from this for human conflicts?

## Anthropomorphic Comparisons

While elephants are animals, their learned behaviors—instinctual or taught—mirror human socialization. In the Serengeti, conflicts are life-and-death decisions. Humans, similarly, are shaped by their upbringing, peer influences, and social environments. How we respond to peer pressure and how we draw our boundaries as young men and women often define our future decisions.

- **Key Question:** Is it possible to retrain individuals to think and act as responsible citizens, or will they revert to the immaturity that led them to incarceration?

## Recognizing the "Elephant in the Room"

Discuss with your instructor and peers: What are the behaviors that lead to criminal acts? Can you acknowledge that your thinking and choices have contributed to your current situation?

- **Self-Review:** What triggers your anger? How do you respond when you are upset, both mentally and physically? Veterans and retirees will challenge your thinking and test whether you can move beyond old patterns of thinking and adopt new problem-solving strategies. This will require more than avoiding consequences, it involves retraining your instinctive responses, both mentally and physically.

**The Importance of Change**

Your ability to manage conflict depends on your trained responses. Will you choose to behave as a responsible citizen of Illinois, or will you revert to criminal thinking? The choice is yours.

**Curriculum Goals**

This curriculum is designed to guide instructors, retirees, and veterans in teaching Psychology 101-404 to help you understand that conflict resolution is key to becoming a productive citizen. The author of this program, having served 28 consecutive years in prison, knows what works and what doesn't. Unless you admit that your past actions were misguided and allow yourself to be retrained, you may not succeed in this program or in handling future conflicts.

**Conclusion**

This is just the beginning of your journey toward understanding conflict resolution. Through the study of psychology and human behavior, you will learn to manage your anger and other challenges that may arise as you work toward restoring your citizenship. The choices you make will determine whether you succeed in becoming a restored, productive citizen of Illinois and this country.

---

## MORGUE LIFE IMPACT PROGRAM

1. **Death: What Does It Mean to Me?**
   - **a.** Each participant is required to write what death means to them and how death is valued in our society.
   - **b.** Participants will discuss their understanding of death and the value of life with veterans, retirees, and instructors.
   - **c.** Exercises related to the purpose and value of life, as well as the right to live fully with respect and dignity, must be demonstrated. These may include, but are not limited to:
     - Videos of young boys and girls facing terminal illnesses.
     - Stories of gunshot victims paralyzed due to gang violence.
     - Accounts from veterans who were paralyzed or lost limbs in service to their country, alongside reflections on the camaraderie they share with fellow service members.
2. **Guest Speakers:**
   Police officers (current or retired), firemen, and ambulance technicians are encouraged to visit participants and share their experiences witnessing death firsthand and how these experiences changed their lives.

3. **Personal Reflection on Death:**
   Each participant is encouraged to openly discuss with instructors and peers their personal experiences with death—whether within their family, neighborhood, or life in general.
4. **Near-Death Experiences:**
   Participants will share any close calls they've experienced that "almost" took their lives. This reflection will help create awareness of their own mortality and the value of life.
5. **The Value of Life:**
   Participants will explore the question: "What would life be like without each participant?" This exercise simulates the real-life experience of reading obituaries or hearing news reports of deaths in the community, emphasizing that each participant is a member of society, and their death would be a loss to the community.
   - This part of the Morgue Life Impact program aims to help criminal thinkers recognize their value and the value of others, highlighting that every individual facing life and death choices is important.
6. **Written Reflection:**
   Participants must write how each of the above parts (1–5) applies to them personally. Veterans, retirees, and instructors will guide these reflections based on their own experiences.
7. **Discussion on Violence and Justification:**
   Participants are asked to reflect on and discuss their views on violence:
   - Why do they believe killing someone could be justified?
   - Under what circumstances, if any, is violence acceptable?
   - Do they believe they have the right to hurt others?
   - Have they ever played video games that felt like real life?
   - Have they fantasized about hurting others, kidnapping someone, or seeking revenge?
   - Is revenge justified?
   - **For the Instructor:** This part of the program aims to discern bravado from genuine understanding of the consequences of violence. Participants must submit written responses, which will be discussed in groups. The goal is to help them understand the seriousness of their actions and how they affect others.
8. **Death Demonstration: Hope**
   - **Scenario:** A young girl named Hope dies from a stray bullet. Hope represents the future, and her loss symbolizes the many children lost to violence.
   - Participants will be shown videos or films depicting gang violence that results in the deaths of children, demonstrating how white, Black, and Hispanic gangs retaliate against each other, often with innocent children caught in the crossfire.
   - The aim is for participants to see and feel the tragedy of these deaths and reflect on the value of human life, particularly that of children.
   - Participants are expected to express empathy and sadness in response to the violence and death they witness. If a participant fails to demonstrate these emotions, it may signal a deeper issue that requires attention.
9. **Accountability and Reflection:**
   - Each participant must write or type responses to instructors' inquiries and address them as Mr., Mrs., or Miss, respectfully.

- o This reflection is critical to the program, as participants who continue to hold devalued views of life or maintain gang ties may be removed from the program.
- o The program enforces strict compliance with the plea agreement, which includes renouncing gang activity and its associated people, places, and behaviors.
- o **Instructor Responsibility:** Instructors, veterans, and retirees must ensure that participants are serious about change. Allowing responses that reflect bravado or gang loyalty without challenging them undermines the goals of the program. As a test, instructors may isolate known gang members in a room under surveillance to determine if gang ties persist. This helps assess the sincerity of the participants' commitment to change.
- o

10. **Rule Violations:**

- If any instructor, veteran, retiree, professor, or staff member of IDOC witnesses violations of the rules or plea agreement—such as gang activity—staff must prepare a 454-incident report confidentially and submit it to the program administrator with supporting evidence.
- The chief administrative officer will determine whether the participant should be transferred from the program to a local county jail before being moved to IDOC intake for classification.

11. **Morgue Visit:**

- In groups of no more than 10 participants, participants will visit the local city morgue under the supervision of instructors and IDOC security staff.
- Veterans, retirees, and a mortician will explain the embalming process, body preparation for autopsy, and the related procedures.

## PROGRAM ELEMENTS PROVIDING HOUSING TO PARTICIPANTS

### LOCATION OF HOME SITE

Parcels and lots will be purchased by the State of Illinois, cleared of debris, and prepped for foundation installation. Gas lines and plumbing infrastructure will be flagged and installed where applicable. The removal of debris and site preparation will be carried out through bids advertised via local notices or news reports, which will be open to the community and local unions. This includes the removal of dead trees, stumps, and other debris.

### HOME SITE BUDGET

All materials, conduit, fixtures, and prefabricated parts used in the construction of small homes must be itemized and pre-approved by the host community center supervisor. This includes any materials required for the completion of the home. The project must comply with budgetary constraints set by grant funding, infrastructure awards, and the Federal Rehabilitation Act, and must not exceed fiscal appropriations.

The budget must adhere to code regulations and cover materials for the following:

- Land and lot preparation, including parcel preparation prior to foundation installation
- Foundation work
- Framing
- Roofing
- Interior drywall or installations
- Interior trim
- Electrical installations, including conduits prior to foundation installation or pouring
- Plumbing and pipe installations (water, sewer, etc.)
- Cabinetry
- Appliances and fixtures
- Heating and cooling systems, including venting applications
- Special features related to, but not limited to, solar electric and hot water system installation and maintenance
- Backfilling, grading, and horticultural applications for raised gardens and landscaping
- Scrap wood fencing installation, if applicable

*Note:* Scrap wood obtained from lumber yards, donations, or local contractors involved in deconstruction projects (such as flipping homes) should be used for cabinetry prefabrication on-site at community centers, as well as for fencing or other home fixture needs (e.g., bed frames, chairs, furniture, etc.).

## TRANSPORTATION OF PREFABRICATED PARTS AND CONCRETE TO PARCEL OR LOT FROM COMMUNITY CENTER

Union members from all affiliated unions related to their respective module training will participate in this program. Union members will be contracted at reasonable fees to transport prefabricated parts and concrete to parcels of land or lots designated for small homes. Including unions in the program is essential, as they form the backbone of organized labor and the trades that participants are learning and becoming certified in.

Organized labor will be contracted through a bidding process on a rotational basis, with different unions being selected every two years to meet the transport needs for modular buildings. These unions will transport the prefabricated parts to the build sites, using cranes or other necessary equipment to facilitate transportation and construction. This rotational opportunity for union members will be overseen by the community center's superintendent and the Secretary of State's Fiscal Responsibility Office.

The relationship between community members and this program is critical to the success of the participants, ensuring a fair, just, and equitable sharing of financial opportunities. The program's goals must align with the needs of the participants, and any deviation from these objectives will not be acceptable.

## BUILDING TRADES TRAINING MODULES

Complete curricula will be adapted from existing approved sources, including the National Center for Construction Education and Research, or similar.

**Modules include:**

- Concrete Foundations
- Plumbing
- Drafting and Blueprints
- Heating and Air Conditioning
- Welding
- Window and Fixture Installation
- Electrical Application and Maintenance
- Solar Installation and Maintenance
- Horticulture

## MODULARIZATION APPROACH TO SMALL HOME BUILDING

**Modularization Design** is a building approach that offers a flexible, repeatable, or modifiable system to suit the needs of small home designers. Several advantages are associated with this approach:

- Builders can start with a basic module and add modules as needed, depending on finances.
- Modules allow designers to mix and match elements to best meet the needs of the small homeowner.
- Modules can be arranged in a wide variety of floor plans.
- Modules enable small homes to be designed efficiently, adapting to specific terrains.
- Modules allow small homes to be designed efficiently while accommodating groups of various sizes, even if the homes are designed differently.
- A modular approach allows a small home to evolve as the owner lives in it or as family needs change. Small homes can expand as needs grow.

An example of incorporating green elements into the modular design is best demonstrated by the modern use of off-grid shipping containers as small homes. The Restorative Justice Outside the Inside program will utilize the most appropriate solutions for the program's needs, considering cost-efficiency and the incorporation of off-grid applications that meet code requirements for participating communities.

An example is shown in **Fig. 1** below: a prospective small home plan using a 20-foot shipping container as an energy- and money-saving technique to build a prefabricated small home. Features include 160 square feet with a half kitchen, half bath, sleeping space for two, and reliance on off-grid components.

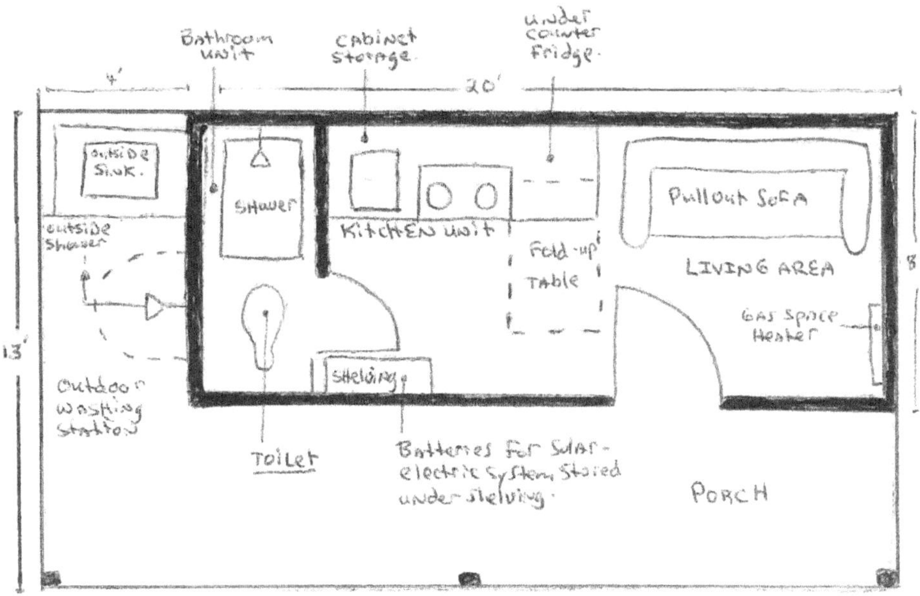


**Figure 2** presents a prospective example of a small home with a 10-foot-high ceiling, which makes the 200-square-foot interior feel much larger. A full-sized Murphy bed folds up against the wall during the day, increasing the usable living space. The home is equipped with solar panels, allowing it to be used off the grid when needed. Its dimensions allow off-site construction, after which it can be trailered to the designated lot or parcel. Key features include 200 square feet of living space, a full kitchen, a three-quarter bath, and sleeping accommodations for two.

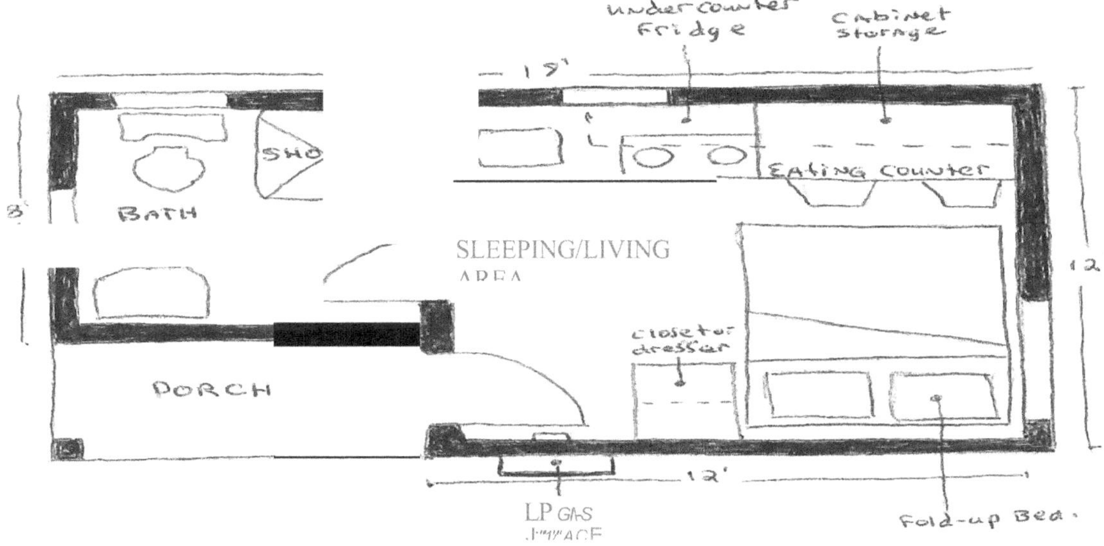

Fig. 3
This compact small home configuration easily sleeps 2 and with a pull-out sofa can accommodate up to four with two closets 2 rows of kitchen cabinets and other storage options it also offers plenty of room for stowing belongings it features 313 square feet a three-quarter kitchen and a half bath.

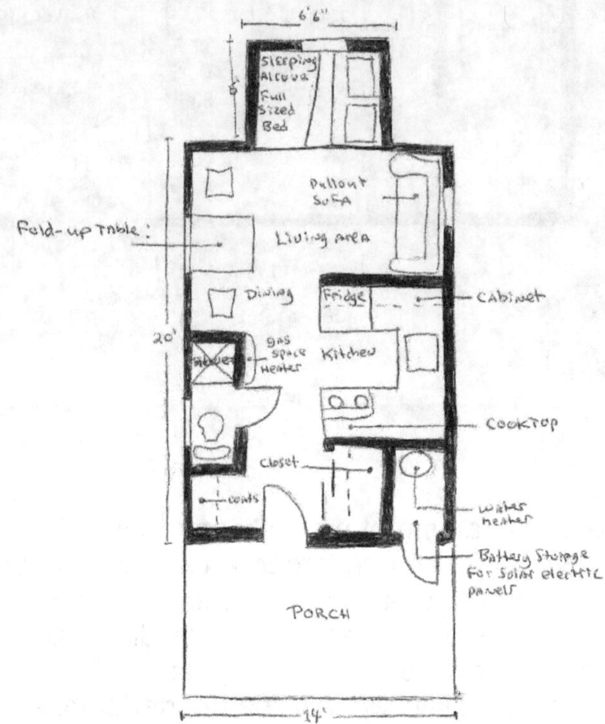


Figure 4: This example of a tiny home is complete with a half bath and kitchen. The space is small but compact and efficient in cooling and heating and energy savings. Features 192 square feet, hall kitchen, half bath, sleeps 1 to 3, and relies on RV components (adaptable).

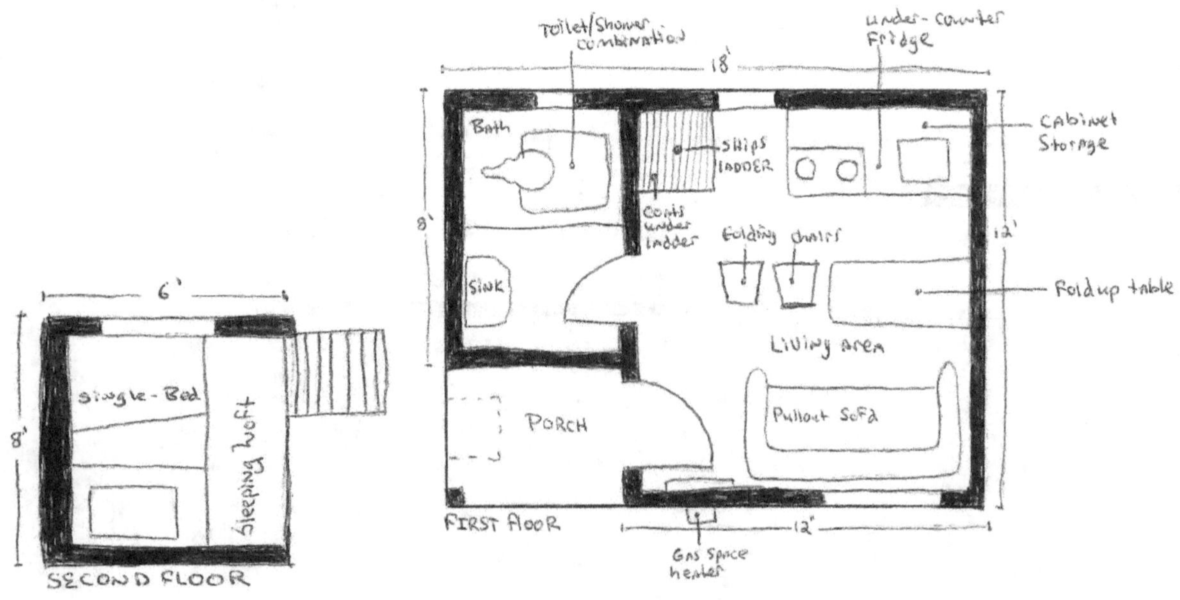

Fig. 5. This small home plan has a first floor of only 144 square feet, but with the addition of a second floor, it feels larger than it appears. The home is designed to be easily heated and cooled, making it energy efficient. With a total of 240 square feet, it includes a hall kitchen and a half bath and can sleep 2 to 4 people comfortably. The design relies on RV components and is built to accommodate off-grid living, incorporating both solar and wind energy systems.

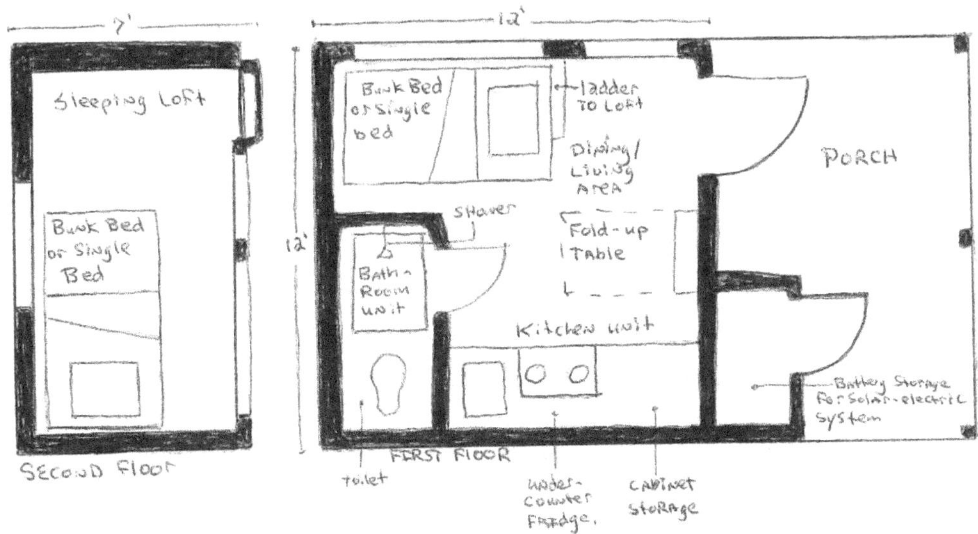


## LOCAL BUILDING CODES

Local ordinances are a controlling factor in home design. For example, cedar shakes for roofing and siding may not be permitted in areas prone to forest fires. In some regions, specific aspects of foundation pouring must be witnessed by city building code inspectors, and the installation of walls, windows, and solar systems must all comply with code regulations.

Business instructors, retirees, and veterans will assist participants in understanding and interpreting code regulations, particularly regarding the installation of concrete foundations, walkways, and slabs required for home completion. It is also essential to guide participants in understanding how to file blueprints and design small homes in compliance with code requirements.

Mastery of blueprint drawing, configuration to scale, and design is crucial for each participant. They must be able to read and create home designs, as well as mechanical and architectural scale drawings for homes, fixtures, foundations, windows, doors, outlets, and more.

## GREEN BUILDING

"Green building" is a term and a new mantra in architecture. Small home designers and builders should always consider "off-the-grid" power systems, which are key components of green building, as follows:

- **Low environmental impact:** Building in harmony with nature, rather than in opposition to it.
- **Energy efficiency:** Creating well-insulated, low-energy-consuming buildings.
- **Use of sustainable resources and materials:** Prioritizing renewable materials whenever possible and avoiding hazardous substances such as formaldehyde or ozone-depleting materials.
- **Use of salvaged or recycled materials:** Reusing materials to maximize the energy and resources used in their production.
- **Long-range planning for the good of the planet:** Designing for people and their habitats, including the use of low-maintenance plants and landscaping. Consider water drainage from altered landscape areas (e.g., limiting paved surfaces), which allows water to percolate into the ground.
- **Cost and financial benefits of going green:** Using materials that require little to no maintenance and have a long lifespan.
- **Design innovation:** Recognizing that functionality is key; smaller homes are often more efficient than larger ones.
- **Flexible and recyclable buildings:** Creating buildings that evolve with changing needs, using materials that can be reused or recycled.
- **Supporting local economies:** Purchasing locally produced products whenever possible to stimulate the local economy and minimize the cost and resource depletion associated with transportation.

## WATERLESS OR LOW-WATER-USE TOILETS

Low-gallon-per-flush (low-GPF) toilets save water, energy, and reduce septic system usage. The new low-GPF toilets available today are significantly more efficient than those from just a few years ago.

## HEATING/COOLING SYSTEM MAINTENANCE

Regular, yearly cleaning of all parts of your heating and cooling systems will increase efficiency and reduce energy use. Ensure chimneys, stovepipes (if applicable), and furnace filters are kept clean. Additionally, keep air ducts, radiators, and fans free from blockages, as heat needs to circulate effectively.

## LIGHTING

Today's fluorescent lights are of much higher quality and far more energy-efficient than incandescent bulbs. Light-emitting diode (LED) lighting is another excellent option due to its minimal energy consumption and extremely long lifespan. LEDs are particularly efficient because they produce very little heat—nearly all the electricity consumed is converted into light energy.

## SHADE TREES

One of the best ways to reduce cooling costs in the summer is by planting shade trees. Properly positioned, they block sunlight from hitting your roof. Trees absorb solar energy for photosynthesis, converting it into carbohydrates instead of allowing it to heat your home. In northern climates, deciduous trees are a good choice because they shed their leaves in winter, allowing for solar heating.

## AVOID ENERGY HOGS

Always purchase energy-efficient, Energy Star-rated appliances, even small countertop devices like toasters and coffee makers. Although the savings on electricity may seem small, over the life of the appliance, the cost savings will accumulate. For instance, prisoners in the Illinois Department of Corrections use only one low-energy hot pot for cooking and hot water. Similarly, clothes dryers are energy hogs—consider using a drying rack instead. In the summer, hang clothes outdoors on a line, and in the winter, place the drying rack near a stove or furnace.

Air conditioning is one of the largest energy users in a home. Minimize usage by cooling the space and then turning the air conditioner off. Use solar-powered fans to circulate air within the home. Good natural ventilation and insulation will greatly reduce the need for prolonged air conditioning or heating. Ceiling fans, especially when powered by solar-charged batteries, are a much more energy-efficient alternative and can circulate warm air during winter months. "Sleeping porches" can also help beat the heat without relying on air conditioning.

## INSULATION

Use the highest R-value insulation you can afford during construction. Insulate walls, roofs, attics, foundations, and any openings (e.g., wall switches, outlets, window and door frames). House wrap applied over the wall sheathing during construction will block wind and serve as a moisture barrier. In colder climates, consider windows with a higher R-factor or add storm windows over Thermopane windows to conserve even more energy.

An airtight home is more energy-efficient, though some may find it stuffy. Be sure to insulate your hot water heater and pipes. Many insulation kits on the market are too thin to meet energy needs, so opt for thicker insulation (such as 5¾-inch insulation designed for 6-inch-thick walls). Proper insulation of hot water pipes will reduce heat loss before water reaches the faucet.

## CEILING FANS

Ceiling fans can significantly enhance comfort in a small home while using far less energy than air conditioners. Connect ceiling fans to an off-grid circuit powered by solar-charged batteries. In summer, ceiling fans are an affordable alternative to air conditioning, and in winter, they can be run in reverse to circulate warm air.

## LOWER THERMOSTATS

Heating in small homes should be controlled by a thermostat. Daytime temperatures need not exceed 65 degrees, and at night, it can be lowered to 60 degrees. A programmable thermostat is an excellent option, as it can reduce temperatures at night and return them to normal in the morning.

## PREFABRICATION AND ENERGY-SAVING MATERIALS

Shipping containers offer time-saving construction and can be reconfigured as needed for small homeowners. These homes allow for efficient use of space and energy. Using reclaimed materials such as wood, insulation, windows, and roofing can reduce costs and meet the state of Illinois' green energy savings criteria.

By prefabricating the home at a community site with all modules included, it saves time and money while allowing participants to learn each module as it relates to building codes and small home construction. This also gives participants the opportunity to incorporate their own ideas into the home before it is delivered to their site.

Materials must meet code requirements, but many can be obtained through networking with contractors at deconstruction sites. Items like windows, doors, roofing, conduits, toilets, and piping can often be acquired for free from union contractors. Refurbished furniture and appliances can also help meet the goals of the small homeowner, supported by partnerships with business owners, veterans, retirees, farmers, and union contractors.

## CONCLUSION

My family and I have witnessed a decline in accountability regarding taxpayers' dollars, particularly as it relates to communities, veterans, and retirees having a say in how those tax dollars are most effectively used. My wife and daughter, along with their neighbors and community, were directly affected by crime. They had to move from their home in Illinois because of the increasing crime directly at their doorstep, which was left unaddressed by their legislators in their district.

As a prisoner who has been incarcerated for more than 28.8 years straight, I have seen many inmates leave prison without having access to educational opportunities due to staff shortages, lockdowns, and in-prison oppression related to addiction. They are often released with nothing but the clothes on their backs and frequently return only weeks later because they have no resources or support. Some are released to the homes of family or friends, only to become a burden to them and their community due to their inability to pay for food, clothing, housing, gas, and other bills. They are released as a threat to public safety because of their desperation, lack of skills, and lack of any meaningful experience in taking responsibility for anything in their entire lives.

Building homes and providing training, mentorship, and education from farmers, business owners, retirees, and veterans—alongside local college professors—within a program designed to be cost-free for taxpayers is an incredible opportunity. It not only offers support to crime victims but also gives back to the community. It is my hope and prayer that this program serves as a foundation for our communities, addressing crime in a systemic way by using taxpayer dollars effectively to benefit victims, communities at large, and the individuals within their boundaries.

From the Williams family, God bless.